WOULD YOU RATHER...?

For Kids!

Justin Heimberg & David Gomberg

Published by Seven Footer Press
276 Fifth Ave., Suite 301
New York, NY 10001

First Printing, November 2007
10 9 8 7 6 5 4 3
© Copyright Justin Heimberg and David Gomberg, 2007
All Rights Reserved

Would you rather...?® is a registered trademark used under license from Falls Media LLC,
an Imagination company

Design by Tom Schirtz

Printed in USA

ISBN-13 978-0-9788178-2-4

www.sevenfooterkids.com

Table of Contents

How to Use This Book iv

You've Been Cursed 1

Powers and Fantasies 37

Cool and Unusual Punishment .75

Would You Rather Live in a World Where 121

Getting Personal 133

Would You 145

New School 153

Random Play 167

Make Your Own Questions 207

HOW TO USE THIS BOOK

1) Sit around with a bunch of friends.

2) Read a question from the book out loud and talk about it. You won't believe some of the stuff you'll come up with as you think about which choice to make.

3) Everybody must choose! That's the whole point. It forces you to really think about the options.

4) Once everyone has chosen, move on to the next question.

It's that simple. We have provided a few things to think about for each question, but don't stop there. Much of the fun comes from imagining the different ways your choice will affect your life.

You may want to grab a pencil, as sometimes, you will get to fill in the blank with someone you know or other information. Other times, you will make up your own questions, keep score of who chose what, and more!

Enough jibber-jabber. It's time to enter the wacky world of *Would You Rather...?*

Chapter One

You've Been Cursed!

Here's the deal: For reasons beyond your understanding, your life is about to change. You are about to suffer a terrible curse—something that will change your life forever in all sorts of ways. Luckily for you, there is a silver lining to this dark cloud. You get to choose between two possible fates.

Would you rather...

cough the sound of a bomb exploding

OR

burp the sound of a rapid-fire machine gun?

Would you rather...

walk like an eighty-year old

OR

walk like a two-year old?

YOU MUST CHOOSE!

Would you rather...

CRY HOT TAR

OR

SNEEZE WITH THE FORCE OF A DOUBLE BARREL SHOTGUN?

3

Would you rather...

have eyes that change color
based on your mood

OR

have your eyes always moving
as if watching a ping-pong match?

Things to think about: trying to read, staring contests

Reasons 1st choice is better

_____

_____

_____

Reasons 2nd choice is better

_____

_____

_____

YOU MUST CHOOSE!

Would you rather...

HAVE LIVING EYEBROWS THAT CRAWL ABOUT YOUR FACE

OR

SKIN THAT DOESN'T TAN UPON DIRECT CONTACT WITH SUNLIGHT, BUT RATHER PLAIDS?

Would you rather...

have a nose that throbs
like a human heart

OR

have to use toothpaste
to wash and shampoo yourself?

Take a vote!

Number of people who voted for choice #1: _____

Number of people who voted for choice #2: _____

YOU MUST CHOOSE!

Fill in the Blank!

Would you rather...

be attached at the hip with

_____

(insert someone you find annoying)

OR

have to marry_____?

(insert someone you find horrible)

YOU MUST CHOOSE!

8

Would you rather...

have erasers for thumbs **OR** corkscrews for pinky fingernails?

fish for hands **OR** mops for feet?

licorice for hair **OR** Silly Putty for earlobes?

YOU MUST CHOOSE!

Would you rather...

EAT EVERY OBJECT IN THE
DICTIONARY BETWEEN
"GHOST" AND "GRAY"

OR

BETWEEN
"BLIMP" AND "BROWN"?

Would you rather...

have the voice in your head sound like Jar Jar Binks

OR

President George Bush?

Would you rather...

have glow-in-the-dark freckles

OR

have red smoke always leaking from your nostrils?

YOU MUST CHOOSE!

Would you rather...

HAVE FINGERNAILS THAT GROW AT A RATE OF ONE INCH PER MINUTE

OR

HAVE HAIR THAT GROWS AT THE SAME RATE?

Would you rather...

have 6 lips **OR** 6 fingers?

1 nostril **OR** 8 nostrils?

34 toes **OR** 3 tongues?

How about 10 toes, each one the size of a banana **OR** 1 tongue that is 3 feet long?

YOU MUST CHOOSE!

Would you rather...

HAVE TO SHOWER AND BATHE
DAILY WITH A HIPPOPOTAMUS
(HIPPOPOTAMUS IS NOT
DANGEROUS)

OR

HAVE TO LIVE WITH FORMER
NBA GREAT PATRICK EWING
(EWING IS NOT DANGEROUS)?

Fill in the Blank!

Would you rather...

have 8 _____ s
(insert part of body)

OR

20 _____ s?
(insert a different part of the body)

Things to think about: chores, playing tag, eating

YOU MUST CHOOSE!

Would you rather...

HAVE TO SLEEP EACH NIGHT BETWEEN YOUR MATTRESS AND BOX SPRING

OR

COLLECT LINT AT 10,000 TIMES THE NATURAL RATE?

16

Would you rather...

HAVE AN 8 INCH WIDE INNIE BELLY-BUTTON

OR

HAVE A 10 INCH LONG OUTIE BELLY-BUTTON?

Would you rather...

snore the sound of a dial-up modem

OR

fart the sound of a cuckoo clock?

Would you rather...

have invisible skin

OR

see in strobe light?

Things to think about: _____

_____

_____

YOU MUST CHOOSE!

Would you rather...

ALWAYS HAVE TO WEAR MOONBOOTS

OR

A SOMBRERO?

Would you rather...

be 50 pounds heavier and look it

OR

be 300 pounds heavier but look the same as you do now?

Reasons 1st choice is better

_____

_____

_____

Reasons 2nd choice is better

_____

_____

_____

YOU MUST CHOOSE!

Would you rather always have to wear...

pants two sizes too small **OR** shirts ten sizes too big?

two left shoes **OR** tea bag earrings?

an NFL referee shirt **OR** a wizard's robe and hat?

YOU MUST CHOOSE!

Fill in the Blank!

Would you rather always have to wear...

a hat made of _____

(insert food)

OR

shoes made of _____?

(insert a material)

Things to think about: getting hungry, running, when it gets hot

YOU MUST CHOOSE!

Would you rather...

HAVE WORMS FOR EYELASHES

OR

CORDUROY SKIN?

Would you rather...

have permanent Cheetos stains
on your fingertips

OR

appear as Harriet Tubman
in all photographs?

Things to consider: your birthday pictures, school pictures,
wearing white clothes, holding hands

YOU MUST CHOOSE!

Would you rather...

HAVE MAYONNAISE TEARS

OR

KOOL-AID SWEAT?

Make Your Own
"You've Been Cursed" Question!

Would you rather....

_____

OR

_____ ?

Who chose what:

Name   Choice

_____   _____

_____   _____

_____   _____

_____   _____

YOU MUST CHOOSE!

Would you rather...

BE LIMITED TO CLEANSING YOURSELF BY USE OF A DUSTBUSTER

OR

HAVE HAIR THAT CHANGES COLOR AND FALLS OUT IN THE AUTUMN?

27

Would you rather...

have lit candle wicks for hair

OR

have asparagus for fingers?

Things to think about: sleeping, standing under a sprinkler, writing, nibbling on your fingernails

Reasons 1st choice is better

_____

_____

_____

Reasons 2nd choice is better

_____

_____

_____

YOU MUST CHOOSE!

Would you rather...

drool maple syrup

OR

bleed glue?

Things to think about: no need for stitches, pancake breakfasts

More things to think about: _____

_____

_____

_____

_____

YOU MUST CHOOSE!

Would you rather...

throw up every time you hear your name spoken

OR

sneeze every time someone says the word "the"?

Things to think about: when people sing "Happy Birthday" to you; when your mom is calling you; how often "the" is used

YOU MUST CHOOSE!

Would you rather...

BE A SIAMESE TWIN WITH YAO MING

OR

MINI-ME?

31

Fill in the Blank!

Would you rather...

have _____'s nose
(insert someone you know)

OR
have _____'s hair?
(insert someone else you know)

Take a vote!

Number of people who voted for choice #1: _____

Number of people who voted for choice #2: _____

YOU MUST CHOOSE!

Would you rather...

grow up in the wild

OR

in a Burger King?

Would you rather...

only be allowed to move in "L" shapes

OR

"Z" shapes?

Things to think about: Try it! Do you end up in the same place?

YOU MUST CHOOSE!

Would you rather...

ONLY BE ABLE TO WRITE BY TATTOOING ON YOURSELF

OR

ONLY BE ABLE TO TAKE PICTURES OF YOUR FRIENDS AND FAMILY BY SCANNING THEM DIRECTLY INTO THE COMPUTER?

Would you rather...

have to wear all your clothes inside out

OR

have to always wear your socks on the outside of your shoes?

Would you rather...

foam up with suds and lather like a bubble bath when wet

OR

have moss-covered arms and legs?

YOU MUST CHOOSE!

Make Your Own
"You've Been Cursed" Question!

Would you rather....

_____

OR

_____ ?

Who chose what:

Name   Choice

_____   _____

_____   _____

_____   _____

_____   _____

YOU MUST CHOOSE!

Chapter Two

Powers and Fantasies

It's your lucky day. You are about to be blessed with a magical superpower to rival Superman, Spiderman, and any of the Fantastic Four (though your power might be a little stranger than theirs.) Even better, you have a say in the matter. You get to choose between two options.

Would you rather...

HAVE A TAPE DISPENSING MOUTH

OR

A BOTTLE OPENING NOSTRIL?

Would you rather...

be able to mimic the voice of anybody you meet

OR

mimic the hair?

Things to think about: Whose voice would you want to mimic and when? Whose hair would you want to mimic and when?

YOU MUST CHOOSE!

Would you rather...

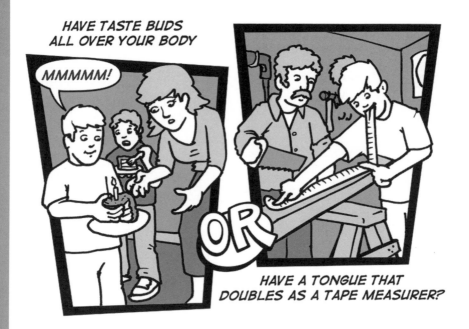

HAVE TASTE BUDS ALL OVER YOUR BODY

MMMMM!

OR

HAVE A TONGUE THAT DOUBLES AS A TAPE MEASURER?

Fill in the Blank!

Would you rather...

go to a dance with _____
(insert someone you like)

OR

have a voodoo doll of _____?
(insert someone you don't like)

Take a vote!

Number of people who voted for choice #1: _____

Number of people who voted for choice #2: _____

YOU MUST CHOOSE!

Would you rather...

BE ABLE TO SHOOT ENDLESS CLING WRAP FROM YOUR HANDS LIKE ICE MAN SHOOTS ICE

OR

HAVE AN EVER-CHANGING TATTOO THAT WORKS LIKE MAPQUEST AND SHOWS YOU WHEREVER YOU HAVE TO GO?

Would you rather...

have a screwdriver outie belly button

OR

a hammer for a big toe?

Things to think about: playing kickball; you'd have to twist your whole body to screw something in; sleeping on your stomach

YOU MUST CHOOSE!

Would you rather...

BE ABLE TO CREATE A JELL-O FORCEFIELD

OR

HAVE SELF-TYING SNEAKERS?

Would you rather...

be able to fast-forward life

OR

rewind it?

Would you rather...

be able to pause the world around you

OR

silence it?

YOU MUST CHOOSE!

Would you rather...

HAVE ROLLERBLADE FEET

OR

TELESCOPING EYES?

Would you rather...

have Gatorade saliva

OR

"toe cheese" that tasted like chocolate?

Who chose what and why:

Name	Choice	Why
_____	_____	_____
_____	_____	_____
_____	_____	_____
_____	_____	_____

YOU MUST CHOOSE!

Would you rather...

BE ABLE TO MAKE CHANGE FOR A DOLLAR BY PUTTING IT IN YOUR MOUTH

OR

BE ABLE TO MAKE AMISH PEOPLE BREAKDANCE?

Would you rather be...

Rash Man (annoys foes with minor skin irritations)

OR

The Tenderizer (softens foes with rapid strikes of a mallet)?

Things to think about: What supervillain would you most want to be?

YOU MUST CHOOSE!

Would you rather...

HAVE A KETCHUP DISPENSING NAVEL?

OR

A PENCIL-SHARPENING NOSTRIL?

Would you rather...

be able to type 80 words per minute with your tongue

OR

be able to toast a piece of bread by staring at it?

Who chose what and why:

Name	Choice	Why
_____	_____	_____
_____	_____	_____

Would you rather...

have an echo that is in the voice of WWE's "The Rock"

OR

have an echo that speaks a second before you instead of after you?

Things to think about: Whose voice would you want to be your echo? What if your echo had an accent?

YOU MUST CHOOSE!

Make Your Own "Powers" Question!

Would you rather....

_____

OR

_____ **?**

Who chose what and why:

Name   Choice   Why

_____   _____   _____

_____   _____   _____

YOU MUST CHOOSE!

Would you rather...

be able to teleport one inch forward

OR

be able to levitate one inch off the ground?

Would you rather...

be able to make yourself 10% invisible (slightly clear)

OR

be able to camouflage perfectly in supermarket aisles?

YOU MUST CHOOSE!

Would you rather...

DROOL DRAIN-O

OR

EXHALE RAID?

Would you rather...

have a servant who carries your stuff around all the time in school

OR

have an expert personal chef?

Would you rather...

have rose-scented body odor

OR

be able to spit 20 feet with pin-point accuracy?

YOU MUST CHOOSE!

Would you rather...

have a lake named after you

OR

have a vitamin shaped in your image?

What would you most want named after you?
Examples: A mountain, a sports move, a dessert, etc.

Name   What he/she wants named after him/her

_____   _____

_____   _____

_____   _____

YOU MUST CHOOSE!

Would you rather...

HAVE RETRACTABLE CLAWS

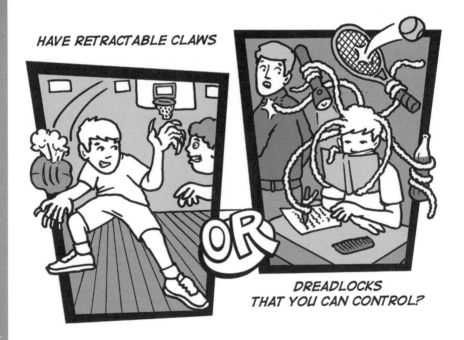

OR

DREADLOCKS
THAT YOU CAN CONTROL?

Would you rather interview...

Bill Clinton **OR** Paris Hilton?

Tiger Woods **OR** Lebron James?

Albert Einstein **OR**
William Shakespeare?

Things to think about: Who would you most want to interview?

YOU MUST CHOOSE!

Fill in the Blank!

Would you rather...

be able to shoot _____
(insert a liquid)
from your eyes

OR

be able to turn_____
(insert an object)
into _____?
(insert another object)

Would you rather...

SEE ABRAHAM LINCOLN AND GEORGE WASHINGTON DEBATE

OR

SEE THEM PLAY A GAME OF ONE-ON-ONE BASKETBALL?

Things to think about: They say George Washington had a 42" vertical leap

Would you rather...

BE A SUPER VILLAIN CALLED "THE PHARMACIST"

OR

THE GOD OF UPHOLSTERY?

WOULD YOU RATHER...? *For Kids*

62

To make golf more exciting, would you rather...

fill bunkers with thousands of fire ants

OR

quicksand?

YOU MUST CHOOSE!

Would you rather...

HAVE A HEAD THAT REFLECTS LIGHT LIKE A DISCO PARTY BALL

OR

PUFF UP LIKE A BLOWFISH WHEN YOU SENSE DANGER?

To make baseball more exciting, would you rather...

put spikes on the outfield wall at baseball games

OR

light the bases on fire?

Things to think about: What change would you make to baseball to make it more exciting?

YOU MUST CHOOSE!

Would you rather...

BE ABLE TO FIGHT BAD GUYS MASTERFULLY WITH YO-YOS

OR

WITH FRISBEES?

Would you rather...

grow up in a Staples office supplies store
OR
a Home Depot?

Reasons 1st choice is better

_____

_____

_____

Reasons 2nd choice is better

_____

_____

_____

YOU MUST CHOOSE!

Would you rather...

HAVE PARMESEAN
CHEESE DANDRUFF

OR

BUBBLE WRAP ACNE?

Would you rather...

HAVE A VELCRO BEARD

OR

AN AFRO OF CRAZY STRAWS?

Would you rather have your dreams written and directed by...

the makers of *Transformers* **OR** *The Incredibles*?

The Wiggles **OR** the writers of soap operas?

the Wayans brothers **OR** the Ringling brothers?

YOU MUST CHOOSE!

Would you rather have on your Instant Message buddy list...

Adam Sandler **OR** Peyton Manning?

Halle Berry **OR** Hillary Clinton?

Cookie Monster **OR** Magneto?

YOU MUST CHOOSE!

Would you rather...

have a dresser that automatically washes, dries, and folds your clothes

OR

have the power to receive and "read" emails in your brain (i.e. without having to use a computer)?

Take a vote!

Number of people who voted for choice #1: _____

Number of people who voted for choice #2: _____

YOU MUST CHOOSE!

Would you rather have the power to....

_____

OR

_____ **?**

Who chose what:

Name   Choice

_____   _____

_____   _____

YOU MUST CHOOSE!

Powers and Fantasies

73

Chapter Three

Cool and Unusual Punishment

Uh oh. You must have done something wrong. Because the fates have decided that you must suffer a horrible experience— a painful challenge, an embarrassing moment, or something else horrific, disgusting, or just generally unpleasant. ☺

Would you rather...

Would you rather...

SLEEP A NIGHT ON
A BED OF PEANUT BUTTER

OR

NEXT TO A HUMIDIFIER
FULL OF VOMIT?

Would you rather...

EAT A SALAD SPRINKLED WITH BOOGERS INSTEAD OF BACON BITS

OR

BE SNEEZED ON BY FIVE ELEPHANTS?

Fill in the Blank!

Would you rather...

have the voice of_____
playing by your bed all night long
OR
have your report card grades
exchanged with _____?

Who chose what:

Name   Choice

_____   _____

_____   _____

_____   _____

YOU MUST CHOOSE!

Would you rather...

BE STONED TO DEATH BY PICKLES

OR

SUBMERGED IN MAYONNAISE UNTIL YOU SUFFOCATE?

Would you rather...

pop a blister and suck out the juice

OR

eat a bowl of Kellogg's scab flakes?

Things to think about: the crunch factor, using a Capri Sun straw

More things to think about: _____

_____

_____

_____

_____

YOU MUST CHOOSE!

Would you rather...

rest your head on a tee and then get smacked with the full-speed swing of a baseball bat

OR

have a bowling ball dropped from twenty feet onto your stomach?

Take a vote!

Number of people who voted for choice #1: _____

Number of people who voted for choice #2: _____

YOU MUST CHOOSE!

83

Would you rather be stuck on an elevator with...

sweaty sumo wrestlers

OR

people who won't stop talking on their cell phones?

Reasons to choose choice #1   Reasons to choose choice #2

_____   _____

_____   _____

_____   _____

YOU MUST CHOOSE!

Would you rather...

BE EXTRUDED THROUGH A SPAGHETTI MACHINE

OR

BE BURIED ALIVE IN A PIT OF PLAY-DOH?

85

Make Your Own Question!
Make up two choices that are painful!

Would you rather...

_____

OR

_____ **?**

Who chose what:

Name   Choice

_____   _____

_____   _____

_____   _____

YOU MUST CHOOSE!

Would you rather...

EAT EVERY OBJECT IN THE DICTIONARY BETWEEN "MOP" AND "MULCH"

OR

BETWEEN "WALLET" AND "YO-YO"?

Would you rather...

eat every object in dictionary between "empty" and "full"

OR

between "tiger" and "trombone"?

Words between "empty" and "full":

_____

_____

_____

Words between "tiger" and "trombone":

_____

_____

_____

YOU MUST CHOOSE!

Would you rather...

FIGHT TO THE DEATH...
15 GEESE

OR

100 PILLSBURY DOUGH BOYS?

Fill in the Blank!

Would you rather...

bathe and powder _____
(insert disgusting friend)
twice a day every day for a week
OR
slap a headlock on _____
(insert friend's mother)
for five minutes?

YOU MUST CHOOSE!

Would you rather fight...

a tiger with no front legs **OR** a rhino with no back legs?

3 possessed lawnmowers **OR** the characters from *SpongeBob Squarepants*?

a real life version of every team nickname of the NFC **OR** AFC?

YOU MUST CHOOSE!

Would you rather...

have your fingernails peeled off,
one by one

OR

fill your pants with raw meat and walk
past a snarling pit bull?

Take a vote!

Number of people who voted for choice #1: _____

Number of people who voted for choice #2: _____

YOU MUST CHOOSE!

Would you rather...

DRINK THE JANITOR'S BUCKET OF WATER AFTER HE'S MOPPED THE CAFETERIA FLOOR

OR

EAT FORTY-FIVE DOLLARS IN NICKELS?

Would you rather...

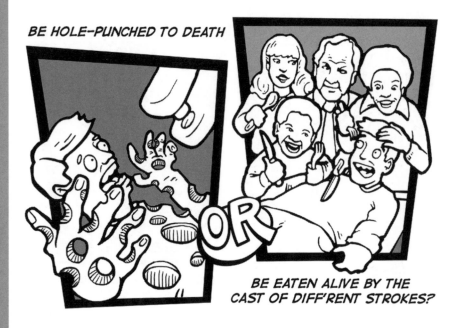

BE HOLE-PUNCHED TO DEATH

OR

BE EATEN ALIVE BY THE CAST OF DIFF'RENT STROKES?

Would you rather...

relax in a Jacuzzi of a stranger's saliva

OR

tongue-clean 10 blocks worth of New York City public phone mouth pieces?

Who said "Ewwwwww!"? _____

_____

_____

_____

_____

YOU MUST CHOOSE!

Would you rather eat...

200 slices of American cheese **OR** 2000 raisins?

14 full sticks of butter **OR** a tennis ball?

all food in liquid form **OR** gas form?

YOU MUST CHOOSE!

Would you rather...

FIGHT A THOUSAND EVIL PIES

OR

A HIGH SCHOOL MARCHING BAND?

I scream, you scream, we all scream (in horror) for ice cream!

Would you rather eat...

a broccoli milkshake **OR** bubble gum ice cream (full of already chewed and spit-out gum)?

salmon sherbet **OR** Dirty Coins and Cream?

ant farm chocolate **OR** dry ice cream?

YOU MUST CHOOSE!

Would you rather eat...

_____ -flavored ice cream
(insert meat)

OR

_____ -flavored ice cream?
(insert vegetable)

Take a vote!

Number of people who voted for choice #1: _____

Number of people who voted for choice #2: _____

YOU MUST CHOOSE!

Fill in the Blank!

Would you rather...

share an eighteen hour car ride with

_____
(insert annoying person)

OR

put on _____ 's
(insert friend)

socks every day for a month?

YOU MUST CHOOSE!

Would you rather...

HAVE YOUR CELL PHONE RING FUNCTION SET ON "AIRHORN"

OR

"TASER"?

Would you rather...

be cooked and hardened into a Shrinky Dink

OR

have your body surgically opened and filled with hundreds of wasps?

Would you rather...

be able to hear every cell phone ring in your neighborhood

OR

smell every fart?

YOU MUST CHOOSE!

Would you rather...

FIGHT 1 VICIOUS WEREWOLF

OR

8 BASHFUL VAMPIRES?

Would you rather...

eat a tarantula

OR

consume, in one seating, three-hundred Three Musketeers bars?

Take a vote!

Number of people who voted for choice #1: Boys _____ Girls _____

Number of people who voted for choice #2: Boys _____ Girls _____

YOU MUST CHOOSE!

Would you rather...

BE MACHINE GUNNED TO DEATH WITH LITE-BRITE PEGS

OR

BE ASSASSINATED BY CABBAGE PATCH DOLLS?

Would you rather...

use an inhaler filled with crushed poison ivy

OR

receive acupuncture with a nail gun?

Would you rather...

nap on a waffle iron pillow

OR

have your tonsils vacuumed out?

YOU MUST CHOOSE!

Make Your Own Gross-Out Question!
Make up two choices that are disgusting!

Would you rather....

_____

OR

_____ **?**

Who chose what:

Name   Choice

_____   _____

_____   _____

_____   _____

_____   _____

YOU MUST CHOOSE!

Would you rather...

BE BEATEN TO DEATH WITH TINKER TOYS

OR

KILLED IN AN AVALANCHE OF D&D DICE?

Would you rather...

109

Would you rather...

experience a brain freeze (literally)

OR

heart break (literally)?

Would you rather...

be used as a human piñata

OR

have your mouth stretched around the part of a lawnmower where the grass spits out?

YOU MUST CHOOSE!

Would you rather be stuck on a desert island with...

Paris Hilton **OR** Harry Potter?

Superman **OR** Aquaman?

_____ **OR** _____?
(insert person who talks a lot)   (insert mean person)

YOU MUST CHOOSE!

Would you rather...

IMPLODE

OR

EXPLODE?

Would you rather never be able to use...

toilet paper **OR** the letter "e"?

a pencil and pen **OR** silverware?

a computer **OR** shoes?

Things to think about: Is there anything you use daily that you could live without? What couldn't you live without?

YOU MUST CHOOSE!

Would you rather...

be shrunken down and live in a land of a Thomas' English muffin

OR

in a bowl of Alpha-Bits?

Things to think about: nooks, crannies, and the third lesser-known and most dangerous crevice type: plelsbons!

YOU MUST CHOOSE!

Would you rather...

DRIP HOT WAX ONTO YOUR EYES

OR

TWIST A CORKSCREW INTO YOUR BELLY BUTTON?

Would you rather...

have Roger Federer forehand your face at full force

OR

have Tiger Woods take a tee-shot to your teeth?

Say that question three times fast.

YOU MUST CHOOSE!

Would you rather...

fight a creature that had the body of a bull and the head of a lion

OR

a creature that had the body of an eagle, the head of a snake, and the hair of Donald Trump?

Things to think about: How would you go about your battle?

YOU MUST CHOOSE!

Would you rather...

fight a creature that had the head

of _____ and the body of
(insert ferocious animal)

a _____
(insert another animal)

OR

a robot that had_____ for arms
(insert weapons)

and a _____ for a lower half?
(insert vehicle)

YOU MUST CHOOSE!

Would you rather...

HAVE AN ALARM CLOCK THAT WAKES YOU UP BY SHAKING YOUR BED VIOLENTLY

OR

BY SLOWLY MAKING THE BED ICE-COLD?

Would you rather...

have an alarm clock that wakes you up by transporting you to a random place in the world

OR

that magically places a gorilla in bed next to you?

Things to think about: What would be the worst way to be woken up?

YOU MUST CHOOSE!

Chapter Four

Would You Rather Live in a World Where...

This time it's the world, not you, that's changing. It could be for the better or it could be for the worse. But any way you slice it, the laws of nature are about to be turned upside-down. And the best part is that you get to decide how!

Would you rather live in a world made of...

pillows **OR** chocolate?

flannel **OR** wicker?

_____ **OR** _____?
(insert anything)   (insert anything)

YOU MUST CHOOSE!

Would you rather live in...

the Star Wars universe

OR

Ancient Egypt?

Take a vote!

Number of people who voted for choice #1: Boys _____ Girls _____

Number of people who voted for choice #2: Boys _____ Girls _____

YOU MUST CHOOSE!

Would you rather...

LIVE IN A WORLD PAINTED BY PICASSO

OR

PAINTED BY A 6 YEAR OLD?

Would you rather live in a world without...

soap **OR** pizza?

telephones **OR** sports?

pants **OR** the Internet?

YOU MUST CHOOSE!

Would you rather...

LIVE IN A WORLD WHERE IT RAINED SUPERBALLS

OR

WHERE PEOPLE HAD MR. POTATO HEAD–STYLE FACIAL FEATURES THAT COULD BE REMOVED AND EXCHANGED?

Would you rather live in a world where...

the moon gave out light like a disco ball
OR
where the sun was the face of your principal?

YOU MUST CHOOSE!

Would you rather...

HAVE SWISS CHEESE LINENS

OR

WALL TO WALL GROUND BEEF CARPET?

Would you rather...

LIVE IN A WORLD COMPRISED ENTIRELY OF NERF

OR

TOOTSIE ROLL?

129

Would you rather live in a world...

where wars were settled with soldiers facing off in massive games of Rock, Paper, Scissors

OR

where you can get out of doing homework by beating your teacher in one-on-one basketball?

Things to think about: What if Shaquille O'Neal was your math teacher?

YOU MUST CHOOSE!

Would you rather...

LIVE IN THE WORLD OF SPONGEBOB SQUAREPANTS

OR

POKÉMON?

Chapter Five

Getting Personal

It's your turn to run the show. For the questions in this chapter, you may need to fill a blank with the name of a friend. Or maybe the name of an enemy. Or something else that only you can imagine. Don't blame us for this chapter. It's *your* warped mind that's responsible for these deranged dilemmas.

Would you rather...

share a bedroom with _____
(insert someone you do not like)

OR

have to kiss _____ every day?
(insert someone you think is gross)

Would you rather...

have to use _____'s
(insert disgusting person)
dirty clothes as a bath towel

OR

drink a cup of _____'s
(insert another disgusting person)
sweat?

YOU MUST CHOOSE!

Would you rather...

have the power to make people _____
(insert an action)

OR

be able to change your body to the size of a _____?
(insert noun)

Would you rather...

be able to transform your head into the head of a _____
(insert animal)

OR

transform your body into a
_____?
(insert household appliance)

YOU MUST CHOOSE!

135

Would you rather have on your Instant Message buddy list...

_____
(insert someone from history)

OR

_____ **?**
(insert a movie character)

Take a vote!

Number of people who voted for choice #1: _____

Number of people who voted for choice #2: _____

YOU MUST CHOOSE!

Would you rather...

have _____ and _____ as your parents
    (insert teacher)   (insert teacher)

OR

have your parents as your teachers?

Things to think about: goofing off, nightly dinners, who's stricter?

YOU MUST CHOOSE!

Would you rather...

make the sound of a _____
(insert animal sound)
when yawning

OR

make the sound of _____
(insert loud sound)
when farting?

Things to think about: _____

_____

_____

_____

_____

YOU MUST CHOOSE!

Would you rather...

_____ was President
(insert schoolmate or friend)

OR

_____ ?
(insert another schoolmate)

Would you rather...

sleep in a bed filled with _____
(insert type of insect)

OR

have your _____ surgically removed
(insert body part)
and then added to your mother?

YOU MUST CHOOSE!

Would you rather...

be caught in a hail storm of _____ s
(insert candy)

OR

swim in an ocean of _____ ?
(insert liquid)

Who chose what and why:

Name   Choice   Why

_____ _____ _____

_____ _____ _____

_____ _____ _____

YOU MUST CHOOSE!

Would you rather...

brush your teeth with toothpaste made
from mashed _____
(insert body organ)

OR

have to bathe with 100 _____
(insert animals)
who lick you clean?

Would you rather...

have a tattoo of _____ on your belly
(insert person or thing)

OR

have the same hair cut as

_____ ?
(insert anyone you want)

YOU MUST CHOOSE!

Would you rather...

work as a crash test dummy

OR

a _____ ?

(insert horrible job)

What bad jobs did you come up with?

_____

_____

_____

_____

_____

YOU MUST CHOOSE!

Would you rather live in the world of...

_____
(insert video game)

OR

_____ **?**
(insert another video game)

Would you rather...

have all your secret thoughts about
_____ posted on Yahoo's home page
(insert crush)

OR

have all your arguments with

_____
(insert family member)

shown on the nightly news?

YOU MUST CHOOSE!

143

Chapter Six

Would You...

The authors of this book are feeling lazy. So lazy, that we didn't even bother to write "rather." The result: a whole new type of question where the answer is a simple "yes" or "no." No problem, right? Guess again.

Would you... get rid of the first letter of your name to improve all your grades by one letter grade?

Would you... wear your Grandma's clothes to get an extra $50 per week allowance?

YOU MUST CHOOSE!

Would you... permanently chain a penguin to your leg to be the King of the city in which you live?

What would be the first law you would pass?

_____

_____

Would you... wear a rainbow colored clown wig whenever playing sports to be 25% faster than you are now?

YOU MUST CHOOSE!

Would you... eat a live cockroach sandwich for $5,000?

What is the grossest thing you'd eat for $5,000?

_____

_____

Would you... go to school in nothing but your underwear for chance to meet _____ ?

(insert favorite singer)

Who said yes?
For which singer? _____

YOU MUST CHOOSE!

Would you... give up 8 inches of your height if it meant your parents could never again tell you what to do?

Would you... allow a dentist to remove all your top teeth with no anesthesia to meet Justin Timberlake and star in his next music video? If not, is there anyone who would be worth it?

_____

_____

YOU MUST CHOOSE!

Would you... spend 2 weeks
locked in a room with _____
(insert worst person you know)
for unlimited credit at _____ ?
(insert favorite store)

Would you... bathe in a tub
of vomit for a free Nintendo Wii and all
of its games?

Would you... drink a glass of
a stranger's spit for front row seats to
the next Super Bowl?

YOU MUST CHOOSE!

Would you... put a live rat in your mouth to have your biggest crush fall madly in love with you?

Would you... eat a tennis ball for $1000? If not, how much would you eat one for? _____

YOU MUST CHOOSE!

Chapter Seven

New School

Due to the rising costs of education, your parents were forced to send you to a *different* school. Your school's rules don't apply here. Don't get too excited, though. There are all kinds of "new rules" to deal with. But unlike in your school, you get the ultimate choice.

Would you rather...

your desk chair buck like a bronco

OR

your pencil squirm and slither like a snake?

Would you rather...

have pencils that can write in any font at regular speed

OR

be able to erase the chalkboard by thought?

YOU MUST CHOOSE!

Would you rather...

HAVE TO SLEEP IN MEDIEVAL ARMOR PAJAMAS

WEAR BRAVEHEART-STYLE FACE PAINT WHEN AT SCHOOL?

Would you rather...

your teachers be clowns **OR** shepherds?

romance novelists **OR** dog trainers?

professional wrestlers **OR** weathermen?

YOU MUST CHOOSE!

Would you rather...

be sent to detention where you are forced to watch 6 straight hours of *Teletubbies*

OR

where the principal gives you a swirly (he sticks your head in a toilet and flushes it) and then sends you home?

YOU MUST CHOOSE!

Would you rather...

the classrooms at your school be
4 feet by 4 feet by 4 feet

OR

be gravity-free?

Take a vote!

Number of people who voted for choice #1: Boys _____ Girls _____

Number of people who voted for choice #2: Boys _____ Girls _____

YOU MUST CHOOSE!

Would you rather...

go to a school where your teachers direct all questions in class to you

OR

where you're given twice as much homework as the other students?

Take a vote!

Number of people who voted for choice #1: Boys _____ Girls _____

Number of people who voted for choice #2: Boys _____ Girls _____

YOU MUST CHOOSE!

Would you rather...

GO TO A SCHOOL WHERE YOU'RE REQUIRED TO WEAR OUTFITS FROM LORD OF THE RINGS

SCOOBY DOO?

Would you rather...

have a teacher that teaches in rap

OR

Piglatin?

Things to think about: Which teacher would you most want to see rap?

YOU MUST CHOOSE!

Would you rather...

HAVE TATTOOS OF VARIOUS GEOMETRIC FORMULAS

OR

ALL OF THE US VICE PRESIDENTS' HEADS?

Would you rather...

go to a school where relentless *Terminator*-like hall monitors roam the corridors with paintball guns looking for students without hall passes

OR

where kickball games were refereed by drill sergeants?

YOU MUST CHOOSE!

Would you rather...

your school bus be replaced with an extended bicycle built for 20

OR

get dropped off at school by a large hawk?

Things to think about: the view from above, who's driving the bike.

YOU MUST CHOOSE!

Would you rather...

your cafeteria serve leeches with tomato sauce

OR

juice boxes filled with the collected underarm sweat from the New Jersey Nets after a basketball game?

Things to think about: Is it any worse than what they are serving now?

YOU MUST CHOOSE!

Chapter Eight

Random Play

Would You Rather...? is on random play. And when we say "random," we mean really RANDOM! There's no telling what kind of question will be asked: a curse, a torture, a power? And there's no limit to the obscenely odd, absolutely absurd, grotesquely gross situations you might be faced with.

Would you rather...

have your eyes and ears switch places

OR

your nose and belly-button?

Things to think about: wearing glasses, what you'd smell, iPod headphones

YOU MUST CHOOSE!

Would you rather...

BE A SIAMESE TWIN CONNECTED AT THE SOLES OF YOUR FEET

OR

AT THE LIPS?

Random Play

169

Fill in the blank!

Would you rather...

be a Siamese twin connected at the

_____

(insert body part)

OR

connected at the _____?

(insert another body part)

Things to think about: playing doubles tennis, eating, having a girlfriend or boyfriend

YOU MUST CHOOSE!

Would you rather...

have your name changed to
Sir Smellsalot

OR

Patty McDoodoo?

Would you rather...

have to write everything with lipstick

OR

cake frosting?

YOU MUST CHOOSE!

Would you rather...

ONLY BE ABLE TO EAT ORANGE FOODS

OR

ONLY BE ABLE TO EAT FOOD STARTING WITH THE LETTER "K"?

Would you rather...

belch the sound of a gong

OR

sneeze the sound of thunder?

Would you rather...

have skin as sticky as a sticker

OR

have a magnetic face?

YOU MUST CHOOSE!

Google Neil Diamond if you don't know who he is.

Would you rather always have to wear...

traditional Samurai garb **OR** a Spiderman costume?

clothes made from pizza cartons **OR** Ziploc bags?

a twenty pound top hat **OR** cross country skis?

YOU MUST CHOOSE!

Would you rather...

HAVE PERMANENTLY LATHERED HAIR

OR

ONLY BE ABLE TO MOVE AROUND BY MOON-WALKING?

Important! This page is very serious and should only be read by well-behaved children.

Would you rather...

produce helium-filled boogers **OR** TNT-filled boogers?

perfectly cubed boogers **OR** glow-in-the-dark boogers?

boogers that randomly pop out like popcorn **OR** boogers that multiply every ten seconds?

Things to think about: Ask the same questions, but with "poop" instead of "boogers".

YOU MUST CHOOSE!

Would you rather...

HAVE A RECEDING HAIRLINE

OR

A PRO-CEDING HAIRLINE?

Would you rather share a lunch table with...

The founding fathers **OR** Transformers?

NBA all-stars **OR** The X-Men?

The authors of this book **OR** Martin Luther King, Jr.?

YOU MUST CHOOSE!

Would you rather...

be made of Lego blocks that could be rearranged

OR

be made of Stretch Armstrong material?

Things to think about: gym class, stacking yourself taller if you need to reach something, getting punched

YOU MUST CHOOSE!

Would you rather...

have your pockets filled with an infinite supply of Gummi Bears but be incapable of speaking when not wearing one of those pairs of glasses with the fake nose and moustache

OR

have perfect spelling but on Fridays become convinced you are a glass of orange juice and desperately struggle not to spill yourself?

Things to think about: Can you come up with a stranger question?

YOU MUST CHOOSE!

Would you rather...

HAVE 6 LIPS

OR

34 FINGERS?

Would you rather...

end all conversations with the phrase "Ain't no thang!"

OR

be mysteriously compelled to say "ARRR" in a pirate's voice, before every sentence you speak?

Things to think about: phone calls with Grandma, giving book reports

More things to think about: _____

_____

_____

YOU MUST CHOOSE!

Would you rather...

appear as Albert Einstein in the mirror

OR

any time you enter a room, have Darth Vader's theme sound?

Take a vote!

Number of people who voted for choice #1: _____

Number of people who voted for choice #2: _____

YOU MUST CHOOSE!

Would you rather...

VOMIT MARBLES

OR

SWEAT CHEESE?

Would you rather...

any time someone asks you a question
and you don't know the answer,
a thousand artichokes fall from above
onto you

OR

have every object you touch instantly
turn to Sugar Smacks cereal?

YOU MUST CHOOSE!

187

Would you rather...

have a comic book-style thought bubble revealing your thoughts

OR

a comic book-style speech bubble instead of a voice?

Things to think about: loss of privacy, hiding your thoughts with a big hat, being able to talk with the deaf, being unable to talk with the blind

YOU MUST CHOOSE!

Would you rather...

have a permanent "Got Milk" moustache

OR

have small holes in your cheeks that allow fluids to leak through like a strainer?

Reasons to choose choice #1

_____

_____

_____

Reasons to choose choice #2

_____

_____

_____

YOU MUST CHOOSE!

Would you rather...

FIZZ UP LIKE ALKASELTZER WHEN IN THE WATER

OR

HAVE A WRITTEN LISP?

Would you rather...

only be able to exit buildings through the window

OR

only be able to enter through the window?

Who chose what and why:

Name   Choice   Why

_____   _____   _____

_____   _____   _____

_____   _____   _____

YOU MUST CHOOSE!

Would you rather...

BE STUCK ON A STALLED BUS WITH FORLORN ACCOUNTANTS

OR

NOSY PIRATES?

Would you rather...

go to a school where the school uniforms were superhero costumes

OR

where dodgeball and math were combined into one class?

Things to think about: your math teacher, getting hit while trying to solve a word problem

YOU MUST CHOOSE!

Would you rather...

EMIT STEAM FROM YOUR EARS WHEN YOU'RE ANGRY

OR

MAKE THE SOUND OF THE JEOPARDY THEME WHEN THINKING?

Would you rather...

HAVE A COMB-OVER FROM YOUR EYEBROWS

OR

FROM YOUR BACKHAIR?

Fill in the Blank!

Woud you rather...

spend a five hour car ride with

_____
(insert teacher)

OR

be _____ 's slave for
(insert teacher)
a day?

YOU MUST CHOOSE!

Would you rather...

ALWAYS HAVE TO WEAR 28 INCH STILETTO HEELS

OR

CLOTHING MADE FROM LIVE SALAMANDERS?

Would you rather...

have a condition where when you get mad, popcorn starts to pop in your trousers

OR

make the sound of a foghorn when yawning?

YOU MUST CHOOSE!

Would you rather...

notice live maggots in your Milky Way after you've eaten two big bites

OR

find a pile of hairs at the bottom of your Caesar salad?

Who said "Ewwwwww!"?

_____

_____

_____

_____

YOU MUST CHOOSE!

Would you rather have complete control over...

who gets elected president

OR

who wins the Super Bowl?

Things to think about: Who would you elect president?
Who would you make win the Super Bowl?

YOU MUST CHOOSE!

201

Would you rather live in a world...

where it snowed cotton candy

OR

where humans sniffed each other like dogs?

Who chose what and why:

Name	Choice	Why
_____	_____	_____
_____	_____	_____

YOU MUST CHOOSE!

Would you rather...

slide down a banister of razor blades into a pile of Cajun spice

OR

be buried up to your neck and have your head used as a golf tee for a day?

YOU MUST CHOOSE!

Would you rather...

consume a Big Mac, vomit it up, re-cook it and eat it again as sauce for a bowl of spaghetti

OR

replace the vanilla fillings in a box of Oreo cookies with a layer of fat from your thigh and then eat them?

Things to think about: Can you come up with something even more gross?

YOU MUST CHOOSE!

Would you rather...

have a Tic Tac dispensing nose

OR

have rocket thrusters on the bottoms of your feet?

Chapter Nine

Make Your Own Questions!

Okay, so you should have the hang of it by now. But do you have what it takes to write your own *Would You Rather...?* questions? Here's a hint: When in doubt, think weird, gross, embarrassing, cool, or painful. And don't worry; not only are there no wrong answers—in this case, there are no wrong questions!

Make Your Own Super Power Question!

Would you rather
have the power to...

_____

OR

_____ **?**

Things to think about: _____

_____

_____

_____

YOU MUST CHOOSE!

Would you rather....

be able to teleport to _____

(insert time and place)

OR

shoot bullets from your _____ ?

(insert part of the body)

Who chose what:

Name   Choice

_____   _____

_____   _____

_____   _____

YOU MUST CHOOSE!

Make Your Own Super Power Question!

Would you rather ....

_____

OR

_____ **?**

Things to think about: _____

_____

_____

_____

YOU MUST CHOOSE!

Would you rather....

OR

_____ ?

OUCH!

YOU MUST CHOOSE!

Make Your Own Painful Question!

Would you rather...

stick a _____ in your eye
(insert object)

OR

swallow a _____ ?
(insert something sharp)

That hurts!

YOU MUST CHOOSE!

Make Your Own
"You've Been Cursed" Question!

Would you rather....

_____

OR

_____ ?

Take a vote!

Number of people who voted for choice #1: _____

Number of people who voted for choice #2: _____

YOU MUST CHOOSE!

Make Your Own Question!

Would you rather live in a world where....

_____

OR

_____ **?**

Who chose what:

Name   Choice

_____   _____

_____   _____

YOU MUST CHOOSE!

Make You Own Super-weird Question!

Would you rather....

_____

OR

_____?

Take a vote!

Number of people who voted for choice #1: _____

Number of people who voted for choice #2: _____

YOU MUST CHOOSE!

Make Your Own
"You've Been Cursed" Question!

Would you rather....

turn into _____ for one
(insert person)
minute of every hour

OR

turn into a _____ ?
(insert animal)

Who chose what:

Name   Choice

_____   _____

_____   _____

YOU MUST CHOOSE!

Make Your Own Question!

Would you rather live in a world where....

_____

OR

_____ ?

Things to think about: _____

_____

_____

YOU MUST CHOOSE!

Make Your Own
"Cool and Unusual Punishment" Question!

Would you rather....

_____

O R

_____ ?

Who chose what:

Name   Choice

_____   _____

_____   _____

YOU MUST CHOOSE!

About the Authors:

Little is known about authors Justin Heimberg and David Gomberg. Some say they are locked up in a mental institution where they spend all day writing bizarre questions on their cells' walls. Others say they are aliens determined to confuse the planet into chaos. Still others say they are stricken with a bad case of "diarrhea of the imagination" for which no sort of toilet paper has yet been invented. If the last theory is right, look out! They say it's contagious!

About the Deity:

The Ringmaster/MC/overlord of the *Would You Rather...?* empire is "The Deity" (pronounced DEE-it-ee). It is the Deity who is responsible for creating and presenting the *WYR* questions, and it is the Deity who, without exception, proclaims **YOU MUST CHOOSE!** No one knows exactly why he does this. Suffice to say, it is for reasons beyond your understanding. Do not defy the Deity by saying "neither" or refusing to choose, or you may awaken to find yourself plagued with one of his horrible curses for real!

Got Your Own *Would You Rather...?* Question?

Go to **www.sevenfooterkids.com** and submit your question and share it with others. Read and debate thousands of other dilemmas by the authors and other kids.

www.sevenfooterkids.com

Featuring:

New questions and illustrations!

More humor and games!

More funny game books!